KATE
Loyal Wife, Royal Mother, Queen-In-Waiting

By Jessica Long

As a "thank you" for purchasing this book I want to give you a gift. It is 100% absolutely free.

Please go to http://fandomkindlebooks.com/royal-family-bonus/ to discover more fascinating intimate facts about Kate and her life as loyal wife, royal mother, Queen-in-waiting.

Disclaimer

Table of Contents

Introduction

On the 6th September 1997 the World said a final goodbye to Diana, Princess of Wales. Amongst the most touching and enduring images of the day was that of her two young sons, following their mother's coffin through the streets of London.

William and Harry, at just 15 and 12 years of age, were thrust into the focus of the watching World. How would this tragedy affect these young boys on the cusp of manhood?

In the years that followed, the boys were kept largely out of the spotlight. An agreement was brokered between the Royal Family and the press, allowing them to grow up in peace, away from the ever present photographers who had hounded their own mother.

This agreement worked for the most part and interest in the two boys was put on hold while they completed their education.

After finishing his school studies, Prince William decided to continue his education at St. Andrews University in Edinburgh, Scotland. It was here that he met his future wife, Catherine Middleton.

Due to the black-out imposed on the press, they were able to enjoy a courtship away from prying eyes. Safe in the protected circle of their close friends, they were free to get to know each other before the rest of the World knew about them.

Once their University days were over though, it was a different matter, and Kate and William were thrust into the limelight. Everyone wanted to know who this girl was who had seemingly captured the heir to the British throne's heart.

Unsurprisingly, William was extremely cautious about introducing his new love, not only to a waiting World, but also to the world of the Royal family. He was determined not to make the same mistakes he felt had been made with his precious mother.

What followed was a long wait, until he felt ready to make Kate his wife. He refused to be rushed and allowed her as long as she needed to adjust to life under the microscope.

On her wedding day, Kate walked into Westminster Abbey on the arm of her father as a commoner, but walked out on the arm of her husband, as the future Queen of England.

This is her story, how a little girl from Berkshire, England, grew up to find her real life Prince Charming.

Her Childhood

Born Catherine Elizabeth Middleton on the 9th January 1982, Kate was the first child for parents, Carole and Michael Middleton.

Carole and Michael worked for British Airways as a flight attendant and an aircraft dispatcher respectively, and Kate spent her early childhood in Amman, Jordan.

Kate has two siblings. Her sister, Philippa (Pippa) Charlotte, was born on the 9th September 1984, and brother James William on the 15th April 1987.

On returning from Amman, the family settled back into their home in Bucklebury, Berkshire in southern England.

In 1987, when Kate was five years old, her mother, Carole, set up her own business, 'Party Pieces', making party bags for local children.

The business flourished and Michael left his job to help his wife with what was to become a multi-million pound business, selling party decorations and supplies.

Kate attended St. Andrews School in nearby Pangbourne until she was 13.

After St. Andrews, she attended private school (known as public schools in the UK), Marlborough College.

Kate was a sporty girl who enjoyed playing tennis, netball and hockey at school.

She gained 11 GCSE's and 3 A-level's, a significant academic achievement.

It was Kate's great grandmother, Olive Lupton, who was responsible for Kate and her siblings having the private education that they did, and ultimately move in the same circles as Prince William.

Olive Lupton died in 1936 at the age of 55. On her death she set up a trust fund for the family of £52,031 (equivalent to £2.9 million today or $4.85 million).

Kate took a gap year after leaving school and spent part of it in Chile.

Kate decided to further her education at St, Andrews University in Edinburgh, Scotland.

She studied 'History of Art' and achieved a 2:1 (upper second class degree).

Kate's family is incredibly important to her and they are very close. Kate enjoys regular holidays with them, and she and William are frequent visitors to Berkshire.

The Courtship

University Life

William and Kate met at St. Andrew's University in Edinburgh, Scotland, in 2001.

St. Andrew's is Scotland's oldest university, dating back to 1411.

Their paths crossed shortly after starting at St Andrews, as they were both living in the St. Salvato's (known as Sallies) hall of residence.

Rumor has it, though, that William's eye was turned when Kate took part in a fashion show on campus in 2002. Her risqué, see-through outfit may have had an effect and the rest as they say is 'history'.

In their second year at university, Kate, William, and a group of friends moved to 13a Hope Street, a Victorian townhouse in the middle of town.

Their third and fourth years were spent at a secluded property, called 'Balgove Cottage'.

The cottage was situated on the historic Strathyrum Estate, and afforded the young couple with the perfect amount of privacy.

Their personal time at St. Andrews was spent surfing, walking and enjoying one of the many bars and restaurants in town.

Ma Bells and the West Port were particular hangout favorites with the couple, and meals were

had at both the Jahanger Indian Restaurant and the Anstrither Fish Bar.

Kate and William graduated in the Younger Hall at St Andrews in the presence of William's grandmother, Her Majesty, Queen Elizabeth II.

After University

On graduation in 2005, in what has become a royal heir's rite of passage, William left university to pursue a career in the Army and, eventually, as an Air and Sea Rescue pilot.

In January 2006, William began his military training at the Royal Military Academy in Sandhurst.

For Kate, finding a career path after university wasn't so easy. Finding a job that would fit in around William's training and give the couple time to be together, as well as being a suitable job for a Royal girlfriend, took some time.

In November 2006, she took a part-time position as an 'Accessories Buyer' with the retail firm, Jigsaw, in London.

During this time, on her way to and from work, she ran the daily gauntlet of press photographers who were camped outside her flat. It was a sight similar to that experienced by Lady Diana Spencer decades earlier, before her marriage to William's father, Prince Charles.

And then, In April 2007, the World was shocked by reports that William and Kate had split up.

Alleged pressure from the Royal family, over whether to propose to Kate or move on, was cited as a reason for the split.

When William's father was faced with a similar dilemma with Diana, he proposed. William went the other way.

Prince William has since said of the split: 'We were both finding ourselves and being different characters, it was very much (about) trying to find our way and we were growing up, so it was just a bit of space and it all worked out for the better'.

However, within a few months William and Kate were back together, and in September 2007 they flew to the Seychelles (in the Indian Ocean) for some much-needed private time.

Here, in the sunshine and relaxed atmosphere, they made an agreement with each other. For the next few years, they would work and enjoy life as much as they could out of the spotlight.

They came to an understanding (no-one knows how explicit) that at some point in the future they would marry and become one of the focal points of the Royal family.

It was obvious that this young couple would do things their own way.

Back in London, Kate left her position at Jigsaw, and went to work at the family business. This afforded her more privacy and allowed her to back away from being in the public eye.

In January 2010, William moved to RAF Valley, Anglesey, in Wales, to begin work as a 'Search and Rescue co-pilot'.

The couple rented a secluded cottage on the island of Anglesey, and Kate divided her time between here and her family home in Berkshire.

During the years that William and Kate got back together and prior to them becoming engaged, Kate was given the nickname 'Waity Katy' by the British tabloid press, so-called for what they saw as her hanging on to William in the vain hope her would propose.

During a holiday to Kenya, Africa, William finally popped the question and on the 20th October 2010, Kate said 'Yes!'

On the 16th November 2010, the wait was over and the Royal Palace announced to the World that William and Kate were to be married.

Kate's engagement ring was the one that had belonged to William's mother Diana, Princess of Wales. It was in the possession of William's brother, Harry, who had picked it out as a personal keepsake following his mother's death. However, the boys had a pact that whoever married first could use the ring, and happily let his brother have it.

William's decision to use his mother's ring was his way of keeping her memory alive, and allowing her to be part of the whole celebration.

What followed was a series of public engagements to help ease Kate into 'Royal life', ahead of her wedding to the Prince.

The Wedding

The Preparations

With the announcement of the engagement now official, preparations for the wedding were swiftly underway.

On the 23rd November, the Palace announced that the wedding would take place on Friday 29th April 2011, at Westminster Abbey in London.

On December 15th, Queen Elizabeth announced that the wedding day, April 29th 2011, would be a public holiday for the whole of the UK. It was also declared an official public holiday in the British Overseas territories of Bermuda, Gibraltar, Monserrat, the Falklands, Cayman Islands and the Turks and Caicos Islands. The Crown Dependencies of Jersey, Guernsey and The Isle of Man also enjoyed it as a public holiday.

As William is not an heir apparent to the throne (meaning he is second in line to the throne, and not first), the wedding was not a full state affair. This meant that Kate and William had more control over the wedding than they would otherwise have had, and many of the details were left to them to decide upon.

Three sets of wedding invitations were sent out in the name of the Queen. The first list, of about 1,900 names, was for the ceremony in the Abbey. The second list, of about 600 names, was for a luncheon reception hosted by the Queen at Buckingham Palace. The third list, of about 300 names, was for an evening dinner reception, hosted by Prince Charles.

The Venue

Westminster Abbey was founded in 960AD by Benedictine monks, and has been a place of worship ever since. It is known as a Royal Peculiar. This means that it falls under the direct jurisdiction of the Monarchy, and not a Bishop.

The Abbey has been the traditional location for coronations since 1066.

It only became the church for Royal weddings in the 20th century. Prior to that, Royal weddings took place in Royal chapels, notably the Chapel Royal in St James Palace, London or St George's Chapel, Windsor Castle, Windsor.

The Abbey can seat up to 2,000 people.

The Abbey is the final resting place of 17 monarchs, including Queen Elizabeth I. The last king to be buried here was George II in 1760.

There are many famous people buried in the Abbey, amongst them, Sir Winston Churchill and Charles Dickens.

Although there are many people buried under the floors of the Abbey, there is only one gravestone that you are not permitted to tread on. The grave of the Unknown Warrior can be found in the entrance to the Abbey. It is the grave of a young soldier killed on the battlefields of France during the First World War. His identity is not known, but he lies there to represent the "multitudes" killed in what has become known as the "Great War".

Queen Elizabeth The Queen Mother, William's great-grandmother, placed her own wedding bouquet on the tomb of the Unknown Warrior when she married the future King George VI in 1923.

The Wedding Party

Kate was attended by her sister, Pippa, as her maid of honor. She had four other bridesmaids and two page boys.

William asked his brother, Prince Harry to be his best man.

Her bridesmaids were: Lady Louise Windsor, daughter of the Earl and Countess of Wessex (the Earl is the youngest son of the Queen); Margarita Armstrong-Jones, daughter of Viscount and Viscountess Linley (the Viscount is the son of the  Queen's late sister, Margaret); Grace Van Curstem, daughter of Hugh Van Curstem, a close friend of Prince William; Eliza Lopes, granddaughter of the Duchess of Cornwall (the Duchess is the wife of Prince Charles).

The page boys were: William Lowther-Pinkerton, son of William's private secretary, Major James Lowther-Pinkerton; and Tom Pettifer, son of William and Harrys' former nanny, 'Tiggy' Pettifer.

The Wedding Day

The ceremony was scheduled to begin at 11.00am (GMT)

At around 9.00am (GMT) on the morning of the wedding, the Queen announced new titles to be bestowed on the couple. They became the Duke and Duchess of Cambridge, the Earl and Countess of Strathearn, and the Baron and Lady Carrickfergus.

The 1,900 wedding guests arrived at the Abbey as follows: General wedding guests arrived from 8.15am. VIPs such as Governor-Generals and Prime Ministers of the Commonwealth countries, diplomatic corps and distinguished guests arrived from 9.50am.

At 10.15am, Prince William and his best man, Prince Harry, arrived.

Members of foreign Royal families arrived at 10.20am.

At 10.27am, Kate's mother, Carole, and her brother James arrived.

Members of the British Royal family began to arrive at 10.30am.

At 10.40am, Prince Andrew (William's uncle) and his daughters Princesses Beatrice and Eugenie, arrived. They were accompanied by Princess Anne (William's aunt,) and her husband, and Prince Edward (William's uncle) and his wife.

Prince Charles, and his wife, Camilla, Duchess of Cornwall, arrived at the Abbey at 10.42am.

The Queen and Prince Philip were the last guests to arrive at 10.45am.

At 10.51am, Kate broke with tradition and left the Goring Hotel where she had spent the night and morning before her wedding. She traveled with her father to the Abbey in a vintage 1978 Rolls Royce. All previous Royal brides have traveled to their weddings by horse and carriage.

The bridesmaids and page boys arrived at the Abbey at 10.55am.

Three minutes later the bride and her father arrive, and the World catches its first glimpse of the bride in her wedding dress.

An estimated 1 million people lined the route in London, and a massive cheer rang out as Kate stepped out of the car and entered Westminster Abbey on her father's arm, the train of her wedding dress held by her chief bridesmaid, Pippa.

The ceremony lasted seventy-five minutes after which the new Duke and Duchess of Cambridge emerge from the Abbey as man and wife.

As they paused in door of the Abbey, Kate asks William if he is happy, to which he replies, 'Of course, you are my wife'.

A horse-drawn open carriage takes them back through the streets of cheering people to Buckingham Palace.

Other members of the Royal Family followed in more carriages.

At around 1.30pm the couple appeared on the balcony of the Palace with other members of the Royal family. Not one, but two kisses delighted the crowds below.

Following the luncheon reception at the Palace, Prince William drove his new bride back to Clarence House in his father's beloved Aston Martin sports car.

They returned later in the evening for a dinner hosted by Prince Charles.

The Dresses

The designer of Kate's wedding dress was a closely guarded secret that was not revealed until the morning of the wedding.

Sarah Burton, creative designer at the fashion house Alexander McQueen, was finally revealed as the creator of the dress just as Kate stepped from her car in front of Westminster Abbey.

Kate had worked closely with Sarah to design a dress that was both traditional and modern.

The ivory satin body of the dress was slightly padded at the hips, and narrow on the waist, creating a look inspired by the Victorian tradition of corsetry.

The main body of the dress was ivory and white satin that had been especially sourced in the UK by Sarah.

A full skirt complete with small bustle and 9ft train incorporated lace appliqué and had been designed to look like a flower blooming.

The design of the bodice with its floral motifs was in the style of the 19th century, and was Kate's 'something old'.

Kate's 'something new' were the diamond earrings that her parents had bought her for the occasion.

Kate wore a veil which was held in place by a Cartier Halo Tiara made in 1936, and lent to her by the Queen. This was Kate's 'something borrowed'.

The tiara has a band of graduated scrolls set with 739 brilliant diamonds and 149 baton diamonds.

A small blue ribbon sewn into the skirt was Kate's 'something blue'.

To avoid the tiara slipping, as happened to Lady Diana Spencer on her wedding day, Kate's stylists backcombed the top of her hair to create something for the tiara to sit around. They then made a tiny plait in the middle and sewed the tiara to it.

Kate's wedding bouquet was shaped like a shield, and included lily of the valley, sweet William, hyacinth and myrtle. Adhering to Royal tradition, the myrtle was taken from a plant that had been grown from the myrtle plant in Queen Victoria's bouquet. All Royal brides since Queen Victoria have used myrtle in this way.

The other flowers used all hold personal significance for Kate.

Pippa Middleton, Kate's sister and maid of honor, wore an ivory gown also designed by Sarah Burton.

The young bridesmaids dresses were hand-made by Nicki Macfarlane. Designed to 'echo' the bride's dress, they were made in the same fabric and had the same button detail down the back.

All the bridesmaids wore 'Mary Jane' style shoes with a buckle made from Swarovski crystal.

They wore lily of the valley hair wreaths, said to have been influenced by Carole Middleton's headdress at her own 1981 wedding to Kate's father.

For the evening reception, Kate changed into a second dress, also designed by Sarah Burton. The strapless white satin gown had a full circle skirt and embellished waistband. Kate teamed the dress with a cropped mohair cardigan.

The Rings

Since 1923, it has been tradition for Royal brides to include Welsh Gold in their wedding bands.

Kate's ring was made from a small amount of gold that had been presented to the Queen, and was sat in the Royal vaults.

It came from the Clogau Gold Mine in the mountains of North Wales. This goldmine was at its peak of production in the late nineteenth century, but had been abandoned since the early part of the twentieth century.

The Queen gave the piece of gold, which had been in the family for many years, to William as a gift.

William chose not to wear a wedding band.

Evening Reception

The couple returned to Buckingham Palace in the evening for a private dinner hosted by Prince Charles.

The evening reception was for close friends and family of the couple, and after the meal the guests let their hair down on the dance floor.

British singer, Ellie Goulding, performed her version of 'Your Song' (by Elton John) as the couple's first dance.

The evening finished at 3am after a small fireworks party in the garden.

The Honeymoon

The following morning, William and Kate left the Palace for a weekend 'somewhere' in the UK.

The official honeymoon was put on hold as William had to return to work as a Search and Rescue pilot on the Monday.

William and Kate eventually left for a honeymoon in the Seychelles on the 9th May.

Facts and Figures About The Wedding

An estimated 2 billion people, from over 180 countries, tuned in to watch the TV coverage of the wedding.

Over 2.8 billion status updates about the wedding were reported on Facebook from the UK and America alone.

8,500 journalists covered the wedding from London.

Over 5,000 street parties took place across the UK on the day itself.

10,000 flowers were used to decorate both Westminster Abbey and Buckingham Palace.

187 groomed horses took part in the possession.

Inside the Abbey, 8 trees (6 English Field Maples and 2 Hornbeams) lined the aisle.

William and Kate's Relationship

The couple have forged their own way since their relationship started in 2003.

When William wanted to wait for marriage (while other's around him were pushing the agenda forward), it was Kate who put her trust in him, and stood by his decision.

Kate gives William the normality he has always craved.

While she may be glamorous and intriguing, she is known to be also headstrong and confident, and not one to buckle under pressure.

When once told how lucky she was to be dating William, she replied 'he's lucky to be going out with me'.

William enjoys being part of her close knit, happy, and normal family, and the couple spend a lot of time with the Middleton's, both at their family home and on holiday.

'At home' with the Middleton's is the kind of informal bolt hole experience that William never had growing up. If offers him the opportunity to just be himself, something that he relishes. It is obvious that this 'freedom' and 'piece of normality' that Kate gives him is something he loves.

The couple have broken with Royal tradition by alternating their Christmases between the Royal family at Sandringham, and the Middleton family home in Bucklebury.

It is normal, once someone marries into the Royal family, to spend every Christmas at Sandringham, and for in-laws to stay firmly in the background.

However, the couple certainly have other ideas, and try to include the Middletons in Royal life as much as possible.

They were present for the Queen's Diamond Jubilee celebrations, joining the pageant that travelled down the River Thames in 2012, and also took part in the Royal procession at the Ascot horse races in both 2011 and 2012.

When their new son, Prince George, was born in July 2013, it was William who took to the wheel of their car to drive them home. Again this broke with Royal protocol, but he relishes feeling in control wherever it is appropriate for him to do so, and, as William said, it was important for him to do it.

William and Kate may live in a world of privilege, but she helps to keep his feet firmly on the ground. Her normality and stability are a breath of fresh air to him in a life based on pomp and ceremony.

Kate's Role As Queen-in-Waiting

As second in line to the throne, after his father, William will one day take the crown with his Queen Catherine beside him.

This is undoubtedly a long way off, as although the Queen is 88 years-old at the time of writing this book, and embarking on her 62nd year on the throne, she shows no signs of slowing down.

However, when William's military career ended in 2012, and his transition into life as a full-time Royal got underway, Kate's life changed too.

She had a relatively slow introduction into Royal life, but as her 'maternity leave' with Prince George draws to a close, we can expect to see much more of Kate.

She has taken her time to choose those charities that she wishes to become involved in. At present

she represents the following: The Art Room, Action on Addiction, The National History Museum, The National Portrait Gallery in London, East Anglia's Children's Hospice and Place2be.

During her time living in Anglesey, Wales, she was a local volunteer leader with the Scout Association.

Kate has also given her backing to the M-PACT programme (Moving Parents and Children Together), which is currently one of the few UK programs that focuses on the impact of drug addiction on the whole family.

In recent years the British monarchy has scaled down its operations. There are now just seven key figures within the family, or as they are known, 'senior Royals'. These are: The Queen and Prince Philip, The Prince of Wales and his wife (The Duchess of Cornwall), Prince William and his wife (The Duchess of Cambridge), and Prince Harry. When Harry marries, his new bride will join the ranks of the 'senior Royals'.

Kate has a very important part to play in taking the British monarchy forward into the future, and she has already been credited with bringing the Royal family back into favor.

In late 2013, William and Kate, relocated back to London and set up base in Kensington Palace (the old home of Diana, Princess of Wales). With Prince Harry also moving to the Palace, the three now form a new and strong partnership.

The Royal Foundation of The Duke and Duchess of Cambridge and Prince Harry was set up initially by the two brothers, William and Harry.

That its name was changed to include the Duchess of Cambridge speaks volumes about Kate's desire to become actively involved in all areas of Royal life.

Through the foundation, the trio can work on their charitable ambitions with the main areas of focus (for now) being: Young People (particularly troubled youth), Sustainable Development (particularly models which aim to balance the needs of more housing, with the impact on the natural environment), and The Armed Forces (in particular working with those who return from armed conflict with either physical or emotional injuries).

The foundation also helps manage a gift fund that William and Kate set up ahead of their 2011 wedding.

The gift fund supports 26 charities. Both wedding guests and well-wishers were asked to make donations to these charities, instead of buying wedding gifts. All the causes that benefit from the fund were close to the couple's hearts, and reflect the passions and experiences of their lives thus far.

Kate is very much aware that the focus of attention is firmly on her. She never has a hair out of place, and always has a smile on her face.

Such is her popularity that online clothing sites often sell out of stock just hours, sometimes minutes, after she has been pictured wearing something.

She is careful to avoid being labelled as extravagant, and much like William's aunt, Princess Anne, she will often be seen wearing her outfits for a second and third time.

With a Royal tour of New Zealand and Australia planned for April 2014, William and Kate are getting ready to step up their Royal duties. They are stepping out of the shadows of Prince Charles and Camilla, and forging their own way and own style within the Royal family. Moving forward, we can expect to see a different type of Royal family evolving.

Mother To The Future King

On the 3rd December 2012, William and Kate announced that Kate was pregnant with their first child.

The news was announced earlier than they would have liked, as Kate was suffering from acute morning sickness, known as Hyperemesis Gravidarum.

The couple had been staying the weekend at the home of Kate's family in Middleton, when it became clear that Kate was unwell.

William drove her back to London, where she was admitted to the King Edward VII Hospital in Central London for three days.

The rest of the pregnancy progressed without any problems, with Kate making plenty of public appearances, but naturally slowing down towards the end.

At 6am on the morning of the 22nd July 2013, Kate was admitted to St Mary's hospital in the early stages of labor.

Prince George Alexander Louis, arrived later that day (although his name was not officially released until several days later).

Weighing in at 3.8kg (8lbs 6oz) George made his appearance at 16.24 (GMT).

It was some hours until the announcement was made to the waiting World, as the Kate and William wanted some time alone with their son before anyone else knew.

Times had changed. A media wag commented, "Previous monarchs may have had to fight battles in person or wash the feet of the poor. But they never had to cope with Twitter." Times had changed.

Again breaking with tradition, Prince William spent the night at the hospital with his wife and new son.

The following day, Kate's parents, Carole and Michael, arrived at the hospital to visit their first grandchild, ahead of any of the Royal family.

It was insisted that this didn't break with any protocol, and 2 hours later Prince Charles and Camilla arrived. They had been flown 240 miles from Yorkshire, where they had been carrying out a Royal engagement.

It was a poignant moment for Charles, William and George, as it was the first time in over 100 years that three male heirs to the throne had all been together in one room.

All four grandparents left the hospital with huge smiles on their faces, declaring George a most handsome and beautiful baby.

Several hours later, Kate and William emerged from the hospital with their baby son. Following a short press conference, they then went back inside to strap George into his car seat. William then carried him out, and drove  *his wife and new son back to Kensington Palace.*

The birth of the new heir to the throne was announced in the traditional way. An easel mounted by the gates of the Palace held the formal proclamation. The last time it was used to announce a Royal birth was on the occasion of the arrival of Prince William in 1982.

The following day, after a visit from the Queen, the new family headed for the Middleton home in Bucklebury, where they spent some time becoming acquainted.

There were no official photos of baby George. Instead some private photos of him and his parents, taken by Michael Middleton, were released.

Prince George was christened at the Chapel Royal in St James's Palace on the 23rd October 2013.

He was christened by the Archbishop of Canterbury, the Most Reverend Justin Welby.

The christening was kept a small private affair, with just immediate family and godparents in attendance.

His seven godparents were: Zara Tindall (daughter of Princess Anne and cousin of William), Oliver Baker (a university friend of the couple), William Van Cutsem (a childhood friend of William), Emily Jardine-Paterson (a school friend of Kate), Jamie Lowther-Pinkerton (former private secretary to William, Kate and Harry), Julia Samuel (a close friend of Diana, Princess of Wales), and Earl Grosvenor (the son of the Duke of Westminster).

Traditionally, all Royal babies are christened in a 172 year-old gown, first worn by the eldest daughter of Queen Victoria.

Over 30 newborn Royals have worn the same gown, made from Honiton lace and white satin.

However, following the christening of Lady Louise Windsor (daughter of Prince Edward and the Countess of Wessex) in 2004, the original gown was deemed to be too delicate to be used again.

The Queen commissioned an exact replica be made to replace the robe.

It was first used at the christening of James, Viscount Severn (son of Prince Edward).

The two daughters of Peter Philips (son of Princess Anne) have also worn it.

Prince George makes the fourth Royal baby to wear the replica robe.

Prince George was impeccably behaved throughout his christening, which used a font made for the christening of Queen Victoria's first child in 1841, and water from the River Jordan.

Prince George was next seen in public when he accompanied his mother on a Middleton family holiday to the island of Mustique.

His next 'official' appearance will be when he accompanies both his parents on a tour of New Zealand and Australia in April 2014.

At nine months-old he will be the age William was when he joined his parents, Charles and Diana, as a baby on a tour of Australia in 1982.

During the nine months of Prince George's life, we have already seen Kate determined to break with

tradition and bring a more modern approach to parenting a royal.

That she is able to do so has been largely due to her predecessor, Diana, Princess of Wales, who forged a new path for the Royal family with her determination to be a hands-on mother.

We have no way of knowing for sure, of course, how Kate's parenting methods will diverge from tradition but it is likely given her own family life, that of her husband's, and their approach so far that George will have relationships with his parents and, later, his subjects, that are largely informal, closely connected, and happy.

The Diana Influence

Diana, Princess of Wales, single-handedly changed the face of the British monarchy.

She brought the Royal family into the 21st century, and made them more accessible to the British Public.

Known as the 'People's Princess', Diana was empathetic with those around her, able to put people immediately at ease, with a smile or a touch.

She helped to break down the social stigmas surrounding diseases, like Aids and Leprosy.

It was only natural that she would teach her boys about compassion, and show them that they had a life of privilege, which would require them to give something back.

From a young age she took them with her on engagements (often privately) showing them that there was another side to life, and that they were the lucky ones.

The week of her death saw the whole of London, and indeed all of the UK, fall silent. There was such a public outpouring of grief that hadn't been seen before. People felt they had lost a friend, someone they knew and loved.

In the years that followed her death the Royal family continued to change, and it is safe to say that the lessons that they learned from Diana, have shaped the way the monarchy is seen today.

It is not surprising that her sons, William and Harry have grown up to have the same 'personal' touch as their mother.

Thoughtful, caring, compassionate of others and willing to do whatever they can for the greater good.

Any future wife of either boy was/is inevitably going to be compared to Diana. Thankfully William seems to have chosen well and the public have taken Kate to their hearts, in much the same way as they did Diana. Kate has already been credited with the reviving the popularity of the monarchy, breathing new life into its' future, one that many of us will watch with great anticipation!

Conclusion

The British monarchy is on the cusp of something new. The long reign of Queen Elizabeth II has seen the Royal family change in ways she could not have imagined when she took to the throne, as a naïve 24 year old.

She has steered the family through times of great popularity, but also through times when the public thought them pointless and outdated.

Since the death of Diana, Princess of Wales, the Royal family have reorganized and scaled themselves down, in order to become more 'modern' and relevant with the world and public around them.

The office of the Prince of Wales, and both William and Harry, now have Twitter accounts. They understand that social media and technology are the new ways to connect with the public.

William and Kate are playing an integral role in the future of the House of Windsor. By the time they come to the throne the British monarchy will look a lot different than it does today.

It will move more in line with the families of the European Royals: a pared-down version whose role will be to promote the countries over which they are ceremonial rulers, perhaps with less of the pomp and ceremony for which the British Royal family are known.

The informal, inclusive influence that Diana, Princess of Wales exerted will undoubtedly continue with the generation of new 'Royals' that we now see.

William and Kate are in touch with what is important to the people around them. They have shown that they are less willing to be 'molded' into the traditional role for a Royal and more interested in doing things their own way.

They understand that for the monarchy to survive, they need to move with the times, and provide a life of 'service' that is relevant and important to all, not least themselves.

It is certainly an interesting time ahead for the monarchy, and Kate has proved herself more than worthy of the role she has been given. Confident, warm, enthusiastic and above all natural, Kate has risen to the challenge of life in one of the most famous families in the World. And she has done it, seemingly, with ease.

With William by her side the couple can do no wrong, as they steer the Royal family into new waters. Already called the 'People's Princess' for her similarities to Diana, Kate will surely help remold the Royals into the 'People's Monarchy'.

Don't forget to claim your free gift!

As a "thank you" for purchasing this book I want to give you a gift. It is 100% absolutely free.

Please go to http://fandomkindlebooks.com/royal-family-bonus/ to discover more fascinating intimate facts about Kate and her life as loyal wife, royal mother, Queen-in-waiting